D1477487

The Melting Pot

Compiled by Edna Beilenson

Drawn by Vee Guthrie

PETER PAUPER PRESS
Mt. Vernon, N.Y.

THE MELTING POT

A Cookbook of
All Nations

Onion Soup

1 quart soup stock or consommé
1 cup Parmesan cheese, grated
6 medium onions
Butter

Prepare 1 quart of soup stock or 1 quart of consommé according to the directions on the can. Take 1 cup of grated Parmesan cheese and 6 onions. Peel and slice the onions and fry them in a small amount of butter until they are golden brown. Add to the soup stock and bring to a boil. Cheese may be added or served separately.

Vichyssoise

4 leeks
1 onion
1/8 pound butter
5 medium potatoes, sliced fine
1 quart water
2 cups milk
2 cups medium cream
1 cup heavy cream

Slice finely the white part of 4 leeks and 1 medium-size onion, and lightly brown in sweet butter. Add potatoes, and cover with about 1 quart of water and a little salt. Boil for 40 minutes.

Crush and sieve through fine muslin and finish off by adding milk and medium cream. Season to taste and bring to a boil.

Let cool and pass again through muslin and add 1 cup of heavy cream. Let cool. Serve with chopped chives. Serves 8.

Fish en Gelée

4 pounds fresh water fish
   (trout, pike, etc.)
6 tablespoons vinegar
1/4 teaspoon whole pepper
Dash paprika
1 teaspoon salt
2 teaspoons sugar
1 medium onion, finely chopped
1 piece of celery, finely chopped
1 carrot, finely chopped
3 tablespoons raisins
1 egg, well beaten

Clean, slice and salt fish. Allow to stand several hours in cool place. Boil 1 quart water. Add all ingredients, except egg. Add more water if needed to cover fish. Simmer slowly about 1/2 hour. Do not overcook. Remove fish to dish or mold.

Gradually add stock to egg, stirring continually so egg will not curdle. Pour over fish. Allow it to cool to room temperature or let it jell in mold in refrigerator. Unmold to serve, if jellied. Serves 8.

Quiche Lorraine

16 slices bacon, fried and drained
½ pound Swiss cheese, diced
4 eggs   .
1 cup milk
Salt and pepper to taste
1 9-inch pie shell, unbaked

Crumble bacon in bottom of pie shell. Add cheese. Beat eggs with milk, salt and pepper. Pour over bacon and cheese. Bake at 350° about ½ hour or until firm. Serves 6-8.

Rice Fondue

1½ cups rice
1½ cups milk
4 ounces Gruyere cheese, grated
3 egg yolks
Salt and ground black pepper to taste

Grate the cheese into a bowl, add milk and let stand for 2 hours. Cook the rice by your favorite method. While it is cooking put the milk and cheese into the top of a double boiler over hot, not boiling water.

White meat, white wine— RED meat, RED wine.

Stir until cheese has melted. Add egg yolks and continue stirring until sauce is creamy. Add salt and pepper. Turn flame very low to prevent coagulating of cheese. Add warm milk if sauce is too thick.

Keep rice slightly undercooked. Pack into buttered mold and keep hot for a few minutes over boiling water. Turn onto serving dish and pour sauce over it. Serves 8.

Hamburger, Bourgogne

2 pounds chuck, ground
Salt and pepper to taste
2 tablespoons butter
½ cup blanched almonds,
    coarsely chopped
2 cloves garlic, cut in half
1 cup Burgundy

Shape hamburgers and season with salt and pepper. Fry slowly in butter. Remove to platter and keep warm. In butter remaining in pan brown almonds and garlic. When almonds are slightly browned add Burgundy. Bring to boil. Remove garlic and pour over hamburgers. Serves 6.

Duck à L'Orange

1 6-7-pound duck
Salt and pepper
½ cup sugar
1 cup orange juice
2 tablespoons Curaçao
1½ teaspoons cornstarch
½ cup water

Wipe the duck with a damp cloth and rub it with salt and pepper inside and out. Bake at 400° for about 2½ hours. When done, remove duck to platter and keep warm. Remove all fat from roasting pan.

In a saucepan heat the sugar to a dark caramel color. Add hot orange juice. Mix the cornstarch with the water, adding a little water at a time. Pour into sauce and cook until thickened. Add juices from roasting pan and Curaçao. Pour half the sauce over the duck and put the rest into a gravy boat. Serves 4-5.

Potatoes Dauphinois

6 medium potatoes
Butter
Salt and pepper to taste
Garlic
2 eggs, well beaten
2 cups milk
1 tablespoon sweet cream

Peel and wipe potatoes, then cut into fine slices; add salt and pepper. Place the slices evenly in a shallow casserole, previously rubbed lightly with garlic and butter.

Prepare a mixture of beaten eggs, milk and a tablespoon of thick cream. Cover potatoes with this mixture, dot with butter and cook in a very slow oven. Serve immediately, while potatoes are still bubbling. Serves 6.

Crepes Suzette

1 cup flour
½ cup powdered sugar
½ teaspoon salt
1 cup milk
2 eggs
½ teaspoon Brandy
½ lemon rind, grated

Sauce:

½ cup butter
½ cup powdered sugar
Juice and grated rind of 1 orange
¼ cup Curaçao

Mix dry ingredients, add milk and stir. Add eggs, Brandy, and lemon rind, and cook crepes one by one in lightly greased frying pan. Roll. Re-heat in Crepe Suzette Sauce, which is made by creaming the butter, beating in the sugar and adding juice and rind of the orange and Curaçao slowly and carefully.

When ready to serve, arrange pancakes on a warm platter, pour over the sauce, sprinkle with Cognac, and light with a match to produce a spectacular effect.

The most impressive dessert there is, created by Henri Charpentier at the turn of the century!

Ⓘtalian

Luigi, Giuseppi,
And Rosa and Tony ~
We sing and we dance
And we twirl
MACARONI !!

Italian Garlic Bread

2 loaves Italian white bread
½ cup butter
1 clove garlic
1 heaping teaspoon parsley, chopped

Crush the clove of garlic and simmer with melted butter for about 10 minutes, being careful not to let the butter brown. Remove garlic, and add chopped parsley. Cut the loaves in half lengthwise, and drench the cut sides with the melted butter. Place bread in a warm to moderate oven until loaves are heated through. Cut in 2-inch portions and serve hot.

Eggplant al Forno

1 pound chopped beef
1 can tomato paste
1 large can tomatoes
3 tablespoons olive oil
1 medium onion, chopped
1 tablespoon sugar
Salt and pepper
2 cups water
1 large eggplant, cut in thin slices
½-¾ cup Parmesan cheese, grated

Brown chopped meat. In separate pan brown onion in oil. Add tomato paste and simmer 15 minutes. Add tomatoes, water, salt, pepper and sugar. When meat is brown drain off excess fat and add to sauce. Simmer about 3 hours, covered. Stir occasionally.

Fry eggplant in hot oil until golden brown. In baking dish arrange layers of meat sauce, eggplant and cheese. Repeat until dish is filled, ending with cheese. Bake at 375° for 15 minutes. Serves 6 generously.

Stuffed Zucchini Squash

8 medium-size zucchini
4 cups soft bread crumbs
1 medium-size onion, minced
3 tablespoons parsley, minced
3/4 cup grated cheese
Salt, pepper, to taste
2 beaten eggs
3 tablespoons butter

Cut off ends of zucchini; do not pare. Cut in half lengthwise; remove pulp with spoon; combine with bread crumbs, cheese, onion, parsley, salt, pepper, and eggs. Fill zucchini shells; dot with butter; sprinkle with additional cheese. Bake in 350° oven 1/2 hour. Serves 8.

Too many cooks ...

Risotto, Italian Style

2 cups uncooked rice
12 dried mushrooms
2 cloves garlic
2 tablespoons parsley, minced
½ cup olive oil
2 cups canned tomatoes
5 cups hot chicken broth
Salt and pepper
Parmesan cheese, grated

Soak rice in cold water about 30 minutes. Wash dried mushrooms, cover with warm water, and soak about 20 minutes, until soft, then drain and chop fine. Mash the garlic cloves and mix with minced fresh parsley.

In a saucepan heat olive oil, put in garlic, parsley, and mushrooms, and fry gently a few minutes. Add tomatoes, cover, and let simmer 30 minutes. Drain the rice and put into another saucepan with ½ cup broth.

Cook, covered, until the broth has been absorbed, then add another ½ cup, and so on, until rice is tender. Stir in the tomato mixture, season to taste, and cook about 30 minutes longer. Sprinkle with cheese. Serves 8.

A traditional Italian delicacy for family occasions.

SPOIL THE SAUCE

Minestrone

1 onion
6 carrots
3 potatoes
6 celery stalks
4 quarts soup stock
½ cup diced pork
3 tomatoes, quartered
Sage and basil leaves
Parsley
Garlic
1 cup chopped cabbage
Assorted vegetables
Broken spaghetti
Parmesan cheese, grated

Cook lightly in a small amount of olive oil
1 onion and the same amount of carrots,
potatoes, and celery stalks, all having been
cut into rather small pieces. Cover with
broth or soup stock; add pork, tomatoes,
several sage and basil leaves, parsley, and
a clove of garlic. Cook for about ½ hour,
then add cabbage which has been finely
chopped, a few cut string beans, asparagus
tips, zucchini cut in small pieces, and some
fresh green peas.

Cook for 15 minutes more, then add some
broken spaghetti. When the spaghetti is
done the soup is ready to serve. Season to

taste with salt and pepper. Sprinkle grated
Parmesan cheese on top.

Chicken Cacciatore

1 roasting chicken (4-5 lbs.)
6 tablespoons olive oil
Flour
1/2 pound mushrooms
1 onion
1/2 cup white wine
1 small can Italian tomatoes
1 tablespoon Brandy
A few sprigs parsley
1 clove garlic
2 tablespoons butter

Cut chicken in pieces, sprinkle with salt
and pepper, roll in flour and fry in olive
oil until golden brown. Remove chicken
from pan, and to the remaining oil add
mushrooms and chopped onion and cook
until slightly brown. Add wine and tomatoes. Cook 5 minutes and put chicken
back in pan, making sure that it is well
heated through again.

Add Brandy, chopped parsley and garlic.
Cover and cook slowly. When chicken is
tender, add butter. Delicious with rice.
Serves 6.

Veal Cutlet Parmigiano

1½ pounds veal cutlet,
  cut Italian style
1 cup bread crumbs
2 eggs, beaten
3 tablespoons olive oil
2 small cans tomato sauce
1 clove garlic, minced
Salt and pepper to taste
1 small Mozzarella cheese
Olive oil

Brown garlic in 3 tablespoons oil, add tomato sauce, salt and pepper, and cook slowly for ½ hour. Dip cutlets first in eggs and then in bread crumbs. Fry in ¼-inch oil or shortening.

Place cutlets in greased shallow baking pan. Place a slice of Mozzarella on each. Cover with tomato sauce. Bake in medium oven for 15 minutes. Serves 4-6.

Viennese

A waltz in Vienna
Is just like a dream ~
And so is the pastry,
Dripping with cream!

Goulash, Viennese

3 pounds lean beef, cut in 1-inch cubes
6 tablespoons butter
3 cups onions, coarsely chopped
2 large tomatoes, cut in eighths
1½ teaspoons caraway seeds
1½ tablespoons paprika
Salt to taste

Sauté onions in butter in Dutch oven until golden. Remove from pot. Brown meat in butter left in pot. Return onions. Add all other ingredients and cover tightly. Simmer until meat is tender (1½-2 hours). Stir occasionally and add water if necessary. Correct seasoning. Serves 6-8.

Hungarian Chicken Paprika

2 small frying chickens,
  cut in serving pieces
2-3 onions, finely chopped
3 tablespoons fat
1½ tablespoons paprika
Salt and white pepper
½ pint sour cream
1 cup water
2 tablespoons flour

Wash and drain chicken. Sauté onions in fat in heavy skillet until gold in color. Stir in paprika. Add chicken. Sprinkle with salt and pepper. Simmer slowly for about 1 hour. Add water if necessary. Do not overcook.

Gradually add water to flour. Add sour cream. Mix thoroughly and pour over chicken. Bring to a boil and turn off flame.

Serve with freshly boiled broad noodles. Serves 6.

Pot Roast Supreme

4-5 pounds boneless pot roast
2 teaspoons salt
1 large onion, sliced
$\frac{1}{2}$ cup red wine
$\frac{1}{4}$ cup tomato juice
1 tablespoon paprika
1 tablespoon parsley, chopped
1 tablespoon beef extract
1 tablespoon Worcestershire sauce
Pepper
Garlic salt
1 can condensed black bean soup

Brown roast on all sides. Combine all other ingredients, except bean soup, and add to roast. Simmer covered 3-4 hours until tender. Blend in soup and heat. Serves 8.

Veal in Sour Cream

6 slices bacon, fried and crumbled
3 medium onions, finely chopped
3 pounds veal, cut up for stewing
¾ cup water
⅓ cup flour
1½ cups sour cream
Salt and pepper to taste
¼ cup parsley, chopped
½ teaspoon paprika

Sauté onions slightly in vegetable shortening. Add meat and brown slowly. Add water, salt and pepper. Cover and simmer until done (about 1 hour). Stir sour cream into flour slowly and add to meat. Taste and correct seasoning. Heat, but do not boil.

Remove to serving dish and sprinkle with paprika, parsley and crumbled bacon.

Serve with rice or noodles. Serves 6-8.

Paprika Chicken

1 medium-size roasting chicken
2 onions
1 tablespoon butter
1 teaspoon salt
1 teaspoon paprika
1 cup canned tomatoes
1 tablespoon flour

Fry the onions to a golden brown. Add seasoning and tomatoes. Cut chicken into eighths and sprinkle with flour. Add to sauce, cover tightly and cook for about 2 hours.

Stuffed Cabbage

2 pounds round steak, ground
1 large, fresh cabbage
1 cup cooked rice
1 large onion, minced
Sage, salt, pepper
1 can tomatoes
2 small cans tomato paste
3 tablespoons vinegar
2 tablespoons brown sugar
15 bay leaves
3 ginger snaps

Boil cabbage, head down, in covering water. Cook for a few minutes until slightly tender. Separate leaves. Mix together steak, rice, chopped onion, sage, salt, pepper, and about 3 teaspoons paste. Fill each cabbage leaf with a generous helping of the meat mixture, fold like an envelope, and lay in a large roasting pan.

When cabbage leaves and meat have been used up, cover mixture with tomatoes, paste, 1 paste can of water, vinegar, brown sugar, bay leaves and ginger snaps. Cook covered for 3-4 hours. Serves 8.

Note: Stuffed cabbage benefits from being made the day before. Just re-heat when ready to serve. Raisins and prunes may be added to the above recipe.

Potato Pancakes

6 large potatoes, grated
1 large onion, grated
3 eggs, well beaten
2 teaspoons sugar
1 tablespoon flour
1 tablespoon cracker meal
1 teaspoon salt
Pepper

Place the grated potato pulp in a cheese-cloth and press out all excess water. Then put the potatoes into a mixing bowl, add the rest of the ingredients, and mix well.

Have a frying pan very hot with plenty of butter. Pour the batter into the frying pan in thin layers, or drop by spoonfuls, and fry first on one side and then the other until brown and well-done. Serves 8.

Potato Kugel Cup Cakes

¾ cup flour, sifted
3 teaspoons baking powder
2 teaspoons salt
4 medium potatoes, grated
2 eggs
½ cup melted butter

Sift flour, baking powder and salt together. Grate potatoes and drain off liquid.

Beat eggs, add to grated potatoes and mix well. Add melted butter.

Add potato mixture to flour and mix well. Grease and heat muffin tins. Pour cups ⅔ full and bake in a 350° oven about 25 minutes. Makes 1 dozen.

Noodle Pudding

1 package medium broad noodles (8 oz.)
½ cup raisins
2 teaspoons almond extract
½ cup sugar
½ teaspoon cinnamon
Salt
3 eggs
¼ pound butter
2 cups milk

Boil noodles. Strain and run under cold water, to remove excess starch. Add cinnamon, salt, raisins, sugar, extract; then add milk and eggs, which have been beaten together and half of butter which has been melted.

Put remaining butter in a baking casserole. Heat casserole and pour in the mixture. Bake in a 350° oven until golden brown.

Nordic

Ski togs and cookies
And smörgasbord:
Live like a lady
And eat like a lord!

Swedish Meatballs

⅔ cup bread crumbs
1½ cups milk
1 medium onion
4 tablespoons butter
¾ pound beef, ground
¾ pound pork, ground
1 egg
2 teaspoons salt
¼ teaspoon pepper
½ cup Sherry

Soak bread crumbs in milk. Then chop onion fine and cook in 1 tablespoon butter until slightly brown. Add meat, onion, unbeaten egg and seasonings to bread crumb mixture. Mix thoroughly.

Now melt another tablespoon butter or margarine in a skillet. Form small meatballs by scooping up some of the meat on a teaspoon which has been dipped into the hot fat (good Swedish cooks always do this so meat slips off spoon easily). Brown meat evenly. Keep shaking the skillet to make meatballs turn over and over.

When nicely brown and thoroughly cooked, transfer to a plate, add remaining butter or margarine to skillet and fry remaining meatballs.

Now add about ½ cup water to skillet, add Sherry and all the meatballs. Cook gently over a low heat for about 15 minutes or until all the liquid is completely absorbed. Makes 6 to 8 servings.

Finnish Herring Salad

Small can peas
Small can carrots (cubed)
Small can red beets (cubed)
Small jar of herring fillets
2 hard-boiled eggs, chopped
Whipped cream
Sugar
Vinegar

Drain the vegetables (save juices in separate dishes) and mix the vegetables with herring, vinegar (or lemon juice), sugar, and juice of the vegetables. Keep this in the refrigerator until served.

Before serving, garnish with the hard-boiled eggs, and the whipped cream to which some salt and some juice of the red beets (for coloring) has been added. The whipped cream may be served separately as a dressing. Serve on lettuce, garnished with parsley.

Smothered Swedish Chicken

2 broilers, split
Salt
Pepper
Flour for dredging
2 cups heavy cream
2 cups chicken stock

Season broilers with salt and pepper, dredge outside sparingly with flour, and turn over. Heat heavy kettle, pour in 1 cup cream, add chickens. Cook until well browned, turning occasionally, adding more cream if necessary. Cover tightly, cook until tender, and when done, remove to hot platter.

To 3 tablespoons fat remaining in kettle, add 3 tablespoons flour and stir until well blended; add stock and remaining cream slowly. Bring to boiling point, season and strain. Pour over chicken. Serves 4.

Swedish Sprits

1½ cups butter
1 cup sugar
1 egg, well beaten
2 teaspoons vanilla
4 cups flour
1 teaspoon baking powder

Thoroughly cream butter and sugar; add egg and vanilla. Beat well. Add sifted dry ingredients, mix to smooth dough. Force through cookie press, forming various shapes; or roll — cut out and emboss. Bake at 400° about 8 to 10 minutes.

The best sauce is a GOOD APPETITE !!!

Swedish Platter (Pancakes)

2 tablespoons sugar
3 eggs
1/8 teaspoon salt
3 tablespoons melted butter
1/2 cup flour, sifted
1 1/2 cups rich milk
Swedish pancake pan

Mix the batter a few hours before using. Let stand at room temperature, or in a slightly cool place.

Beat the egg yolks with the sugar, salt and melted butter. Stir in, alternately, the flour and milk. Mix well. Let stand in a cool place until ready to use. Then whip the egg whites until stiff and mix into the batter.

Melt a little butter in each depression of the hot pancake pan. Pour or spoon a little batter into each. The cake browns almost at once; turn it and let the other side brown. Lift the cakes to warmed plates, arranging them 5 or 7 on a plate, in a circle; spoon lingenberry preserves in the middle. Sprinkle the cakes with powdered sugar and serve. Makes 2 dozen or more cakes.

Christmas Cakes

3 packages yeast
¾ cup sugar
2 cups lukewarm milk
5¾ cups flour, sifted
¾ cup butter
½ teaspoon ground cardamom seeds
¾ cup citron, chopped
¾ cup seedless raisins
1 egg

Mix the yeast with 1 teaspoon sugar and stir into it about 3 tablespoons of lukewarm milk. Stir in 1 or 2 tablespoons of flour; mix and let stand 10 minutes in a warm, but not hot, place. Mix the rest of the flour with the cardamom seeds and sugar. Melt half of the butter in the milk and add to the flour and sugar. Stir till well mixed, add the yeast, mix and let stand 20 minutes. Mix or knead in the rest of the butter and let stand another 20 minutes.

Turn the dough out onto a well floured board and knead a few minutes. Cut into 3 or 4 equal parts. Work into each some of the finely chopped citron and a few raisins. Form into oblong loaves. Put them on a greased and lightly floured baking tin and let them stand, lightly covered with a cloth, for 10 minutes. Brush the loaves with slightly beaten egg. Bake in 375° oven ½ hour or a little longer. Recipe makes 15 to 20 or more servings.

Danish Apple Cake

1 package zwieback
1 cup sugar
½ cup butter
8 tart apples, pared, cored and sliced
½ cup heavy cream, whipped

Crush or grind zwieback and mix with sugar. Brown butter slowly in heavy frying pan, do not burn; stir into the crumb mixture. Cover bottom of greased casserole with layer of crumbs; pare, core and slice apples and place on top. Repeat layers of crumbs and apples until all are used, finishing with layer of crumbs on the top.

Bake in 325° oven for 1¼ hours, or until crusty. Serve with cream. Serves 8.

Oriental

The spices and mystery
Of the East
Make an exotic
Western feast!

Chinese Rice

1 cup rice
1 green pepper, minced
1 large onion, minced
1 lump fat

Wash and dry rice. Place in skillet with large lump of fat and fry gently, stirring from time to time. When golden brown, add onions and pepper which have been fried lightly in butter. Pour 2 cups boiling water over rice mixture and season. Cover and cook 20 minutes. Serves 4.

Spareribs, Cantonese

4 pounds young spareribs,
  cut into finger size
2 cloves garlic, cut in slivers
6 tablespoons soy sauce
1 cup brown sugar
Salad oil

Heat some oil in heavy skillet with slivers of garlic. Add spareribs and cook about ½ hour. Be careful to keep turning, so that they do not burn.

Add soy sauce. Turn off heat. Sprinkle with brown sugar. Allow to settle, drain and serve hot. Serves 4-6.

Chinese Salad

2 cups bean sprouts, canned or cooked
1½ cups celery, thinly sliced
1 cup radishes, thinly sliced
1 cup unpeeled cucumber, thinly sliced
1 green pepper, thinly sliced
2 raw carrots, thinly sliced
3 green onions, thinly sliced
French dressing
Soy sauce

Combine the vegetables in a salad bowl, moisten with French dressing, then season with soy sauce to taste. Toss until well mixed. Serves 6.

Sweet and Pungent Shrimp

1 pound fresh shrimp
2 eggs
½ cup flour

Remove shells and veins from shrimp and rinse in cold water. Sift flour into beaten eggs, stirring the eggs at the same time, making a smooth paste. Add salt to mixture. Dip shrimp in egg mixture and fry in deep, hot sesame oil.

Prepare Sweet and Pungent Sauce. Add fried shrimp to sauce. Cook for 2 minutes more. Serve immediately.

Sweet and Pungent Sauce

1 tablespoon cornstarch
½ cup brown sugar
⅓ cup vinegar
6 tablespoons pineapple juice
2 teaspoons soy sauce

Put cornstarch and brown sugar in saucepan. Add vinegar, pineapple juice and soy sauce. Bring to boil and simmer 1½ minutes. Serves 3.

Pepper Steak with Tomatoes

1 pound flank steak
1 pound green peppers
1 pound tomatoes
½ pound onions
1 teaspoon each: salt, sugar and
  Gourmet powder
2 teaspoons soy sauce
2 teaspoons spiced black soybeans
2 cloves garlic
1 cup chicken broth
3 teaspoons cornstarch

Trim steak and wipe clean. Slice cross-grained to obtain thin slices 3 inches by 1 inch by ⅛ inch. Cut peppers, tomatoes and onions into eighths. Crush garlic. Mix cornstarch with ½ cup of broth.

The discovery of a New Dish
DOES MUCH

FOR HUMAN HAPPINESS !!!

Sauté garlic in 3 tablespoons hot fat until slightly brown. Stir in flank steak turning on high flame for 2 minutes. Set aside.

Sauté onions and peppers for 5 minutes, then add tomatoes, salt, sugar, Gourmet powder, soy sauce, ½ cup of broth. Cover and cook vigorously for 2 minutes. Add cornstarch mixture. Stir, cover, and simmer 2 minutes. Blend in steak. Serves 6.

Javanese Bamie

½ pound noodles
4 pork chops
4 onions
1 bunch scallions
Garlic
1 bunch parsley
1 white cabbage (small)
1 bunch celery
1 can beansprouts
½ pound shrimp or 1 can shrimp
Soy sauce

Cut all ingredients, meat included, into small pieces. Fry the pork squares until dark brown. Fry the onions separately, and put them with pork in Dutch oven. Add mashed garlic, the other vegetables and shrimp and finally 2 tablespoons of soy sauce. Do not cook too long.

Cook the noodles in boiling, salted water, and add these last. Use spatula to mix. Serve with pieces of lemon and top each individual plate with fried egg. Serves 4 persons generously; add another chop if a fifth portion is desired.

Note: It is important not to overcook this dish, and the vegetables should retain part of their original crispness.

Curry Soup

1 can chicken and rice soup
2 tablespoons sweet butter
1 tablespoon sweet cream
1 can milk
2 green apples
2 small onions
½ teaspoon curry powder

Mince apples and onions finely, and fry in sweet butter until golden brown. Combine chicken soup and milk and bring almost to a boil, add apples and onions, sweet cream and curry powder. Serves 4.

Curried Lamb with Rice

3 pounds lean lamb breast or
    shoulder, cut in cubes
3 tablespoons fat
Salt, pepper, bay leaf
8 whole black peppers
2 small onions, sliced
1 teaspoon parsley, chopped
⅓ cup flour
1½ teaspoons curry powder
2 tablespoons water

Brown meat in hot fat. Cover with boiling water; add onion, parsley, and seasonings. Cover and cook slowly 2 hours, or until meat is tender. Strain stock; reserve 2 cups. Mix flour and curry powder; add cold water and blend. Stir into stock; cook until thick. Add meat mixture. Serve with fluffy steamed rice.

Arabian Meat and Eggplant

1 large eggplant
2 cups brown rice
5 cups water
2 pounds beef or mutton
Saffron, allspice, salt, pepper
⅛ pound butter
Pine nuts

Chop meat finely and sauté in hot butter. Spread a thin layer over the bottom of a large saucepan. Slice eggplant and sauté to a light brown. Lay eggplant over meat alternating with a layer of the meat until ingredients are used up. In 5 cups of water boil all of the condiments a few minutes. Wash the raw rice and spread evenly over the layers of eggplant and meat. Strain spiced water over the rice.

Cook slowly until rice is done. Melt some butter and pour over the rice. Invert onto a large hot platter. Garnish with fried pine nuts and serve.

american

Most of our foods
Stem from far far away,
But a few, just a few ~
From our own U. S. A.!

Roast Thanksgiving Turkey

Dress and clean turkey. Rub inside with salt and pepper. Stuff neck cavity, and fasten opening with metal pins. Fill body cavity loosely with stuffing. Rub skin well with butter or with paste of ½ cup butter, ¾ cup flour.

Place turkey breast side up in open roasting pan. Drip pan from broiler may be used if large roaster is not available. Roast uncovered in slow oven (300° to 325°) 15 to 20 minutes per pound.

Turkey may be placed breast side down for first half of roasting time to allow juice to run down into breast. Baste at 30-minute intervals with melted butter and hot water. When breast and legs brown, cover with brown paper.

Festive Cranberry Mold

4 cups cranberries (1 lb.)
2 cups boiling water
3 cups sugar
Orange rind, grated

Pour boiling water over cranberries and cook about 15 minutes. Add sugar and rind and cook 5 minutes longer. Mold.

Spicy Pumpkin Pie

1¼ cups pumpkin, cooked and strained
⅔ cup sugar
½ teaspoon salt
½ teaspoon ginger
1 teaspoon cinnamon
¼ teaspoon nutmeg
3 eggs, separated
1¼ cups scalded milk
1 six-ounce can (¾ cup) evaporated milk
½ recipe pastry

Thoroughly combine pumpkin, sugar, salt, and spices. Add egg yolks, milk, and blend. Fold in beaten egg whites. Pour into 9-inch pastry-lined pie pan. Bake in hot oven (450°) ten minutes, then in moderate oven (325°) about 45 minutes, or until mixture does not stick to knife. Top with whipped cream.

Deep Dish Apple Pie

Use ingredients as listed for Apple Pie (*see* page 50), with the exception of pastry. Only ½ recipe pastry is needed. Arrange apples and seasonings in a deep baking pan, or in deep individual baking dishes, cover with pie crust, and bake till apples are tender and crust is brown.

New England Boiled Dinner

4 pounds corned beef, brisket preferred
8 small white onions
8 parsnips
8 carrots
8 potatoes
1 cabbage

Wash beef under running water to remove brine. Place in large kettle, cover with water, bring slowly to a boil and cook 5 minutes. Remove scum, cover and let simmer 2½ hours.

Skim excess fat off liquid, then bring meat to a rolling boil; add whole onions, parsnips, carrots and potatoes, and cook gently, uncovered, 20 minutes. Then add cabbage, which has been cored and cut in eighths, and cook 20 minutes longer, or until vegetables are just tender.

Place meat on hot large platter and arrange vegetables around it. Garnish with parsley. Serves 8.

Harvard Beets

2 tablespoons butter
1 tablespoon cornstarch
1 tablespoon sugar
1/4 teaspoon salt
1/4 cup vinegar
1/4 cup water
2 cups beets, cooked and cubed

Melt butter; add cornstarch, sugar, and salt; blend. Add vinegar and water; cook until thick. Pour over beets. Serves 4.

Apple pie without CHEESE Is like a kiss without a SQUEEZE !

Apple Pie

3 pounds tart green apples
1 cup sugar
2 tablespoons flour
⅛ teaspoon salt
1 teaspoon cinnamon
¼ teaspoon nutmeg
1 recipe pastry
4 tablespoons butter

Peel apples and slice thin; add sugar mixed with flour, salt, and spices; fill 9-inch pastry-lined pie pan. Dot with butter. Adjust top crust. Bake in 450° oven 10 minutes, then in 350° oven about 40 minutes. Serves 6.

New England Baked Beans

1½ pounds beans (yellow-eyed are best)
1 teaspoon baking soda
1¼ pounds lean salt pork,
  cut in thin strips
1½ tablespoons dry mustard
1 teaspoon salt
½ teaspoon pepper
2 tablespoons molasses
6 tablespoons sugar
1 medium onion, chopped fine

Soak beans overnight in cold water. Drain. Cover with fresh water and boil ½ hour.

Add baking soda. Boil 15 minutes more. Drain and rinse thoroughly with boiling water. Mix together mustard, sugar, molasses, onion, salt and pepper. Add enough boiling water to cover.

Fill bean pot with alternate layers of beans and salt pork, with strips of pork on top. Pour other mixture over all. Add enough boiling water to fill pot. Cover pot. Bake 8 hours at 250°, removing cover after 3 hours. Add boiling water as needed, but none the last hour. Serves 8-10.

New England Clam Chowder

¾ cup butter
6 small onions, minced
2 pints clams, chopped
4 cups boiling water
4 potatoes, diced
2 tablespoons salt
2 quarts milk
Pepper to taste

Melt the butter and fry onions until golden brown. Add the chopped clams and simmer 5 or 6 minutes. Add boiling water, potatoes, salt and pepper and cook for 30 minutes. Pour in milk, beat, and serve with oysterettes. Serves 8.

Hot Turkey Salad

2 cups cooked turkey or chicken, cubed
1½ cups celery, sliced
½ cup toasted almonds, slivered
½ teaspoon salt
2 teaspoons onion, grated
2 tablespoons lemon juice
1 cup mayonnaise
½ cup Parmesan cheese, grated
1 cup crushed potato chips

Combine ingredients except cheese and potato chips. Toss lightly. Pile lightly into individual casseroles or custard cups. Top with grated cheese and potato chips. Bake in hot oven (450°) 10 minutes. Serves 6.

Hashed Brown Potatoes

3 cups raw potatoes, diced
6 tablespoons butter
1 teaspoon salt
Black pepper

In a heavy skillet, melt butter, then add potatoes and seasonings. Cook until tender. Stir and lift from bottom, so that potatoes will not stick. Add more butter as needed. When brown on bottom, turn out onto serving dish. Serves 6.

Johnny Cake

1 cup sweet milk
1 cup buttermilk
1 teaspoon salt
1 teaspoon soda
1 tablespoon melted butter
Corn meal

Mix ingredients together. Add enough corn meal to make thick batter. Spread upon buttered tin. Bake 40 minutes. Baste several times with pastry stick dipped in melted butter. Break apart to eat. "Johnny" Cake is a corruption of "Journey" Cake, originally used as fare for long journeys.

Baked Virginia Ham

Place ham fat side up on rack in open roasting pan. Do not cover. Bake in 300° oven, without water, allowing 15 to 20 minutes per pound for a large ham; 20 to 25 minutes per pound for a small ham; and 25 to 30 minutes per pound for a half ham. The shorter cooking time in each case is for tenderized hams. Roast meat thermometer registers 170° when ham is done; 160° for tenderized hams.

Ham may be basted during cooking period with honey, syrup from canned fruit or cider. For the last half hour of baking, rub surface with dry mustard and brown sugar moistened with ham drippings. Score fat in diamonds; stick a whole clove in each.

Ham'n Corn Crisps

2 cups ground, cooked ham
1 medium onion, chopped
½ cup parsley, chopped
1 medium green pepper, chopped
1 teaspoon mustard
⅛ teaspoon allspice
1 egg
1½-2 cups corn muffin crumbs
 (3-4 large muffins)
Butter

Brown onion in butter. Mix with ham, green pepper, parsley, mustard, allspice, egg and 1 cup crumbs, which have been soaked in 1 cup of water and drained.

Shape thin patties, roll in more crumbs, and fry in butter till crisp and brown. Or bake mixture in casserole, sprinkled with crumbs and dotted with butter. Bake in medium oven for ½ hour. Serves 6.

Ham Gravy

½ cup raisins
1 cup water
5 cloves
¾ cup brown sugar
1 teaspoon cornstarch
¼ teaspoon salt
Pinch of pepper
1 tablespoon butter
1 tablespoon vinegar
¼ teaspoon Worcestershire sauce

Cover raisins with water, add cloves and let simmer 10 minutes. Mix sugar, starch, salt, pepper, and stir into mixture until slightly thick. Then add the rest of the ingredients and simmer a few minutes before serving.

Baked Chicken, Maryland

2 broilers, 3 pounds each, cut as for frying
Seasoned flour
2 eggs, beaten
Bread crumbs
½ pound butter

Dip pieces of chicken in seasoned flour, then in beaten eggs, and lastly in bread crumbs. Melt butter in baking dish, lay pieces of chicken in melted butter, and bake for 2 hours at 350°, turning chicken once so that both sides are properly browned, and increasing heat to 500° 10 minutes before serving to make chicken crisp. Serves 8.

Boeuf, Creole

4-5 pounds boneless pot roast
1 tablespoon salt
Pepper to taste
1 pint dry red wine
2 tablespoons fat
2 tablespoons flour
Veal knucklebone
1 quart stock or water
1 cup canned tomatoes
1 clove garlic
Dash thyme
½ bay leaf
Faggot (few sprigs parsley, stalk celery and leek, tied together)
5-6 carrots, cut in pieces
12 small onions, browned in a little butter

Lard roast with a little fat, season with salt and pepper and let soak in wine in a refrigerator for 6 hours, turning the meat over several times. Dry meat well and brown in fat that has been heated in kettle. Drain off fat when roast is golden.

Sprinkle flour in bottom of kettle and mix with the brown juice from the roast. Add bone, wine, stock, tomatoes, garlic, herbs and faggot. The meat should be just covered with liquid, no more. Bring to a boil, cover kettle, reduce heat and cook slowly on a top burner 3 to 4 hours, or until roast is almost tender. Remove meat and bone from gravy. Skim off all fat from gravy and strain.

Clean pan and put back meat with carrots, onions and gravy. Simmer 20 to 30 minutes or until tender.

Creole Fried Chicken

1 frying chicken
3 eggs
1/4 cup milk
1 teaspoon white pepper
2 teaspoons salt
3/4 cup flour
2 cups cracker meal

Wash, split and cut the chicken for frying. Season with salt and pepper. Make mixture of eggs, milk and 1/2 teaspoon of salt. Pour the egg mixture over the chicken and let it stand about an hour or two. Roll chicken in flour and cracker meal which have been mixed together. Fry in hot fat 15 minutes. Serves 4.

Jumbalaya

3 cups rice
1½ cups canned tomatoes
1 slice raw ham
1 large onion
1 green pepper
2 cloves garlic
Thyme
1 bay leaf
1½ cups shrimp or crab meat
¾ cup shortening
Salt and pepper to taste
3 cups water

Wash rice until clear. Fry with shortening and onion until brown. Add the meat, shrimp, tomatoes and remaining seasonings. Cook slowly for 30 minutes. Serves 8.

Wild Rice Cheyenne

1 cup wild rice
1 pound hamburger
2 large onions, sliced thin
1 tablespoon butter
1 teaspoon chili powder
¼ teaspoon powdered thyme
Salt and pepper to taste

Wash rice. Cover with 4 cups hot water. Boil 5 minutes. Drain and rinse. Cover with 4 cups boiling water. Boil 20-25 minutes. Drain and rinse.

Fry onion and loose hamburger meat lightly in butter. Add cooked rice and seasonings. Toss lightly. Serves 3-4.

Dixie Corn Fritters

1¾ cups flour, sifted
2 teaspoons baking powder
¾ teaspoon salt
1 egg, beaten
¾ cup milk
1 cup corn kernels, drained
1 tablespoon melted butter
Vegetable shortening

Sift flour, baking powder, and salt together. Combine egg, milk, corn and butter; stir into flour mixture.

Put enough vegetable shortening into frying pan to make an inch layer when melted; heat. Drop batter from tip of large spoon into hot fat and fry 4 to 5 minutes, or until golden brown, turning when brown on one side; drain on brown paper. Makes about 8 fritters.

Louisiana Rum Cream

5 egg yolks
5 teaspoons granulated sugar
Rum to taste
½ pint sweet cream, whipped
1 dozen lady fingers

Beat together yolks and sugar until light and creamy. Add Rum to taste, and ½ pint cream, whipped stiff. Cut lady fingers in half lengthwise and line bowl. Pour in half the mixture, cover with a layer of lady fingers, and then with the remaining cream mixture. Chill in refrigerator for an hour or two before serving. Serves 6.

Quick Southern Pecan Pie

1 cup sugar
¼ cup melted butter
½ cup corn syrup
3 eggs, well beaten
1 cup pecans
1 unbaked pie shell

Mix sugar, syrup and butter, add eggs and pecans. Fill unbaked pie shell with mixture and bake for 10 minutes at 400°, then for 30 to 35 minutes at 350°. Serve either cold or hot. Delicious topped with unsweetened whipped cream.